MENO

The Library of Liberal Arts
OSKAR PIEST, FOUNDER

MENO

PLATO

Translated by
BENJAMIN JOWETT
with an introduction by
FULTON H. ANDERSON

. . . .

The Library of Liberal Arts
published by

Prentice Hall
Upper Saddle River, New Jersey 07458

Library of Congress Catalog Card Number: 51-7881
ISBN 0-02-360770-X

© 1949 by Prentice-Hall, Inc.
A Pearson Education Company
Upper Saddle River, New Jersey 07458

Printed in the United States of America

ISBN 0-02-360770-X

Prentice-Hall International (UK) Limited,London
Prentice-Hall of Australia Pty. Limited, Sydney
Prentice-Hall Canada Inc., Toronto
Prentice-Hall Hispanoamericana, S.A., Mexico
Prentice-Hall of India Private Limited, New Delhi
Prentice-Hall of Japan, Inc., Tokyo
Pearson Education Asia Pte. Ltd., Singapore
Editora Prentice-Hall do Brasil, Ltda., Rio de Janeiro

CONTENTS
. . . .

INTRODUCTION

The *Meno* is described by Walter Pater as the "most characteristic dialogue of Plato." John Stuart Mill calls it a "gem" among Platonic works, and most aptly, for in no other dialogue of Plato are there exhibited within comparable compass so many facets as the *Meno* contains. The piece is composed about the time when Plato founds the Academy, and it is quite possible that it may be designed—as a learned commentator has suggested—to pose the basic questions for discussion in this institution of learning, which is to determine the mode of Western thought and teaching for many centuries. The dialogue belongs to the "middle" period of the author's writing. During this stage of his reflection Plato is greatly concerned with matters which bear on the education of mankind. The work is preceded by the *Protagoras,* the *Hippias Minor,* and the *Gorgias,* three dialogues in which the author is preoccupied with the relation between technical training and moral wisdom. It is followed, perhaps immediately, by the *Republic,* several of whose doctrines it introduces—sometimes in identical words common to the two. Its treatment of knowledge and training in virtue is partly retrospective, partly exploratory. It instances doctrines which appear in the aforementioned dialogues, and introduces those opinions of the sophist Thrasymachus which are to be delineated fully in the *Republic.* It foreshadows a sharp distinction between sense and reason, a cleavage between opinion and knowledge, the contention that virtue is a function of the human soul, and the assignment of *forms,* such as justice, courage, and temperance, to a noetic world beyond the vicissitudes which beset particulars in time and place.

The scene of the *Meno* is an out-of-doors place—perhaps a street—in Athens. The properties are a bench and a stretch of earth on which Socrates sketches geometric figures. The characters are four. There is Socrates, courteous, modest, patient, with a civilized recognition of what is of worth in his interlocutors. As usual he professes ignorance of the profundities of human nature and conduct, which, he believes, have not yet been plumbed by the mind of man. His intellectual brilliance and resiliency serve to make the drama one of the most swift-moving among Plato's many works.

Socrates' questioner is Meno, who gives the work its name. The dialogue opens abruptly without salutation or other observance of Athenian amenities. Meno is a Thessalian, relatively young, well-born, wealthy. His bearing is somewhat arrogant, as befits his high station among a semi-barbarous people. He is petulant when crossed in discussion and menacing when cornered in argument. He comes from an equestrian people, eager in warfare, precipitous in decision, adventurous always, generous in hospitality, and aware only to a rudimentary degree of moral and political principles. Meno is shortly to assume the command of a division of Greek mercenaries in an expedition of Cyrus the Younger against Artaxerxes II; and it is not improbable that this is the business which has brought him to Athens.

The Thessalian has had education. He knows some poetry, some mathematics, and some philosophy of an Empedoclean sort. Of late the sophist Gorgias has been among his people and has brought to them—along with its many implications—the art of rhetoric. This art, which Gorgias has long professed, the Thessalians believe to be a training in "virtue," even if the sophist himself has on occasion denied that it is.

Sometime during the conversation between Socrates and Meno there appears upon the scene a "family" friend of the latter. This is Anytus, an active Athenian politician and an energetic man. He has a very great respect for the "worthy" citizens of Athens. All innovators he holds under suspicion, and he opines that none of his friends would think of consorting with intellectuals. He himself recognizes no distinction between the sophists and Socrates. When Socrates observes in his presence that the sons of certain renowned Athenians turn out badly or feebly, presumably because their parents do not know how to educate them, Anytus peremptorily issues him the warning that it is not well so to talk about illustrious persons: and significantly, because it is this very Anytus who is to be one of Socrates' accusers at his trial for corrupting the young, by introducing new notions about man's dealing with himself, his fellow citizens, and the gods.

The fourth character is Meno's attendant Slave-boy. The Slave at first sight—to quote an editor—appears hardly "a character, but an abstraction, a typical blank mind." Yet he is to become the representative agency of deliverance from convention to actuality, from a shadowy realm dominated by the changing dogmas of opinion to being itself assured and attested in knowledge.

These are the four speaking characters. Over the scene, however, like destiny in a tragedy, hover two unseen forces. These are in the end to send Socrates to his death. Anytus is the visible symbol of one and Gorgias the invisible token of the other. Anytus represents the *de facto* accusers of Socrates at his trial before an Athenian jury. He will on that occasion speak for the politicians. One Meletus will represent the poets, and Lycon the rhetoricians. Socrates has castigated these three groups for their ineffectual instruction of the Athenian public.

The unseen Gorgias belongs to a band of sophists. As teachers of the young they have become the accredited representatives of the great public. Many condemn them, but the young flock to them for instruction, so commonly that one of their number, Protagoras, has by practising his "art" for some forty years made more money than Phidias the decorator of the Parthenon and ten other sculptors besides. These sophists consider the public a kind of unthinking animal. They teach their pupils how to quiet it, when to rouse its clamors, and how to cater generally to its whims. Their directions in these conjunctions determine the purpose and the limit of their attempts to educate the future leaders of Athens.

The plot of the *Meno* is a disquisition—within the context
of contemporary thought and action—on the question whether
or not virtue can be taught. It takes the form of paradox:
virtue is knowledge, and therefore teachable; there are no
teachers of virtue, therefore it cannot be taught. The problem
is one bequeathed from the earlier *Protagoras*. It is only par-
tially resolved in the *Meno*. The dialogue contains no definition of virtue; this is left for the *Republic*. The Thessalian's
attempt to define objects prove abortive. Trained as he has
been in the sophistic tradition, he confuses enumeration of
instances with the statement of an essential nature.

Throughout the argument of the work Plato brings to bear
on the question of training in virtue thoughts which have
to do with three views of education. His reflections on these
reach a climax about the time he composes the *Meno*. This
is the main reason why this dialogue is to be regarded as one
of the most crucial among the author's writings. The dialogue
moves faster, perhaps, than any other composed by Plato.
The succinctness of its statement of doctrine can scarcely be
paralleled in his other works. Fortunately for the reader, its
doctrines and the perspectives which accompany them are set
forth leisurely and fully in the dialogues which precede and
succeed it.

The three educational practices which Plato brings under
this rapid review are (1) traditional teaching, (2) the "new"
training of the sophists, and (3) his own account of education.
Traditionally the training of the Athenian youth has been
based upon music and gymnastic. His body has been disci-
plined by exercises designed to produce not brute strength
and heavy muscles but a co-ordinated activity at the bid of
his mind. His mind has been informed through the teaching
of the poets, persons "inspired" by the gods. Homer, chief
among these, has provided the Greeks with a holy and au-
thoritative writ. Through the recitation of his verses discipline
and dogma have come to the young. And for their elders, too,
he has been the recognized authority on practices which include, to mention but a few, virtuous conduct, care of the

wounded, military strategy, and political procedure. Following a training in poetry, and in grammar and elementary mathematics besides, the Athenian youth has traditionally been brought into close association with his father or some other person versed in the ways of political practice; and after a relatively prolonged period he has been deemed ready to take his place in the public assemblies.

On this educational procedure, of whose inadequacies not a few Athenians are vaguely aware, Plato makes definite comments. The great Homer and lesser poets attribute to Greek heroes and gods deeds which are a shame to men. Some of the poets, Theognis for instance, when they come to portray weighty matters contradict themselves. The popular Simonides, whose work Meno apparently knows, describes justice as the paying of debts. He thus conceives righteousness as a kind of *quid pro quo,* after the fashion of a business enterprise in which one gets something equivalent in return for what he has given, be this good or evil. Along with Homer he considers it high morality to do good to friends and harm to enemies; and it never occurs to either of the two that they should provide means whereby the real friend and the real enemy may be distinguished from the seeming friend and the seeming enemy. To attempt to do so would, of course, raise difficult questions, and one is not surprised that they overlook these, since poets generally never seem capable of exposing the meaning of their own sayings.

As for Athenians who stand high in political life, they, according to their own confession, have never discovered what either justice in particular or virtue in general is. Actually most of them have never bothered to inquire. The result is that their sons prove inadequate when confronted with the tasks of adult citizenship. The son of Themistocles, for example, and the sons of Pericles have turned out to be skilled horsemen and nothing more.

Of late years there has grown up in Athens and elsewhere a band of "new" teachers called sophists. They are of a general type, but have not grown into a school with identical or

common convictions. They take full advantage of prevalent
misgivings about education. They profess to make training
"scientific," and undertake to provide an educational short-
cut by discipline in the rules of an "art." This art, they say,
can be mastered in a series of lessons. It is their substitute for
long and arduous growth in perception through association
with those long experienced in the intricacies of public and
private life.

The sophists go from city to city. Some of their number
are without roots in any community or civilization. They remain perpetual aliens, and feel free to annihilate in criticism
all conventions and institutions whatever form these may take
and wherever they may be found. Many of these teachers are
not at all concerned with theoretical matters, and are content
to keep to their "art." Practically all of them give political
instruction in some sense or other. Yet at the same time they
refuse to determine the nature of justice. Many of them assume that they are teaching virtue; but they show a disin-
clination or incapacity for defining its character or probing
the depths of human nature whose function it is.

Most of them hold that morality is a conventional business,
differing from age to age, from city to city, from authority to
authority. Extremists among them, pressing a distinction between nature and convention, go so far as to assert that morality is the destroyer of natural capacity. Founded in compacts,
as they say, among the many who are weak, its office is to
thwart the activity of nature's nobleman, the individual strong
in appetite, shrewd in calculation, and resourceful in his
predatory endeavors.

As a class, however, the sophists take but scant cognizance
of moral questions. They are satisfied if in the assemblies their
pupils gain victory over rivals. This is the purpose of their instruction, and they consider themselves superb in attaining
it. They compare themselves to other experts, in medicine,
shoemaking, flute-playing, and the like, and reiterate that education is an "art" (*techne*) to be practiced by experts.

Of their number, perhaps, the best known is Protagoras. He

undertakes to teach his pupils how to manage their public and their private affairs. The instruction he gives is difficult to descry. Certainly he does tell those who associate with him that the end of action is pleasure. He warns them that they are not to be taken in by the immediate pleasures of sense, but are to restrain themselves in the presence of the solicitation of the present moment in order that they may be enabled to enjoy the satisfaction of a greater pleasure in the future. He also asserts that knowledge is opinion founded in sense-perception, and that any individual with any opinion at any time and in any circumstance is the measure of right and wrong.

Another well-known sophist is Hippias. He has appeared at the Olympic games, exhibiting clothes and utensils made by himself, and professing the skill to instruct in all arts and sciences. He is a polymath of sorts who identifies enlightened conduct with the sum of the arts from shoemaking to history. Plato deals with him in summary fashion. While Plato acknowledges that life would be more efficient and more comfortable than it now is were one to dwell in a city in which all the arts were well plied, he also observes that in such a community, unless a moral directive beyond the various techniques of the several arts were provided, there would be nothing to restrain the expert accountant and doctor from stealing the goods and destroying the lives of citizens. By a greater skill which is given through training in the arts man may become the more effective in the pursuit of evil. Technical knowledge is not equivalent to moral wisdom.

Then there is the venerable and persuasive Gorgias, the most famous among the teachers of rhetoric. He has never pretended to instruct in virtue—even if his pupils have assumed that he has taught them this—but only in the art of speaking well. Nevertheless, his educational practices have grave implications. He admits to Socrates that, so great is his power of persuasion, he has been able to convince persons that they should take medicine which without his exercise of rhetorical skill they would have refused. He brags that his well-trained pupils also are able to produce in high degree a condition of belief and consequent action on any matter in the minds of their public. Socrates retorts that Gorgias' rhetoric is like the skill of a pastry cook who, through the concoction of fine sauces, can make food which would otherwise be deemed unpalatable appear good. He then points out the danger for society which lies in a demagogue's power to produce a state of credulity in his hearers. Gorgias bluntly refuses to take the blame for any evil consequences which may follow from the practice of his art. Like a boxing-master, he trains his pupils well; and if, he explains, like skilled pugilists, they go about assaulting citizens, that is none of his business!

Another group of sophists is exemplified by Thrasymachus. These are quite prepared to accept what Socrates considers the immoral implications of the sophistic regime. Indeed, they delight in that conduct of their pupils which Socrates most dreads. They are thoroughgoing immoralists, so much so that they consider justice, as it is understood and practiced, a vice, the token of the weakness of human beings in the mass. They identify virtue and art, and define the latter simply as technical rule. They draw the inference from their definition that no artist ever makes a mistake. Art as such is infallible. That is to say, for example, when a doctor fails to employ and apply the rules of medicine, and acts in error, he is at that time no doctor at all but a potential murderer. When the performer who professes musicianship plays wrong notes, he is then no musician but a noise-maker. Having so described the arts, including the political art which he professes to teach, this type of sophist goes on to assert that the end of political conduct is to get as much goods as possible from the public, "fattening" them, if necessary, in order to fleece them. The "natural" leader who can employ the sophistic art effectively will be able to crash through all religious, political, and moral conventions, and escape by virtue of his strength all unpleasant consequences. Conventions are nothing more than compacts, protective devices made by the many who are weak to be broken by the few who are strong.

Socrates acknowledges the "cleverness" which Thrasymachus shows in his elaboration of the definition of art in terms of technical skill. But he is not impressed by the later stage of Thrasymachus' argument, because in this the sophist deserts a position which he has already affirmed, by confusing the art of money-making and procuring worldly goods with the art of governing. To illustrate: the collecting of fees by the doctor cannot, according to Thrasymachus' definition, be of the essence of the art of medicine. Indeed, it has nothing at all to do with medicine. A doctor's becoming wealthy or remaining poor, as the case may be, is altogether irrelevant to the exercise of his technical skill. What is more, in the practice of art a common objectivity in dealing with subject matter must prevail. All things, according to the sophist's account, which fall under an art's technique, be they bodies, musical sounds, persons, are necessarily governed equally and without exception by its rules. The trained musician who happens to be "stronger" than his fellows does not, when he exercises the art of music, "outdo" them by tightening his strings beyond the proper pitch or by playing more loudly than they. Thrasymachus' politician, technically trained as he presumably is, and defined in terms of the political art, would be like a doctor who, because he had medicine at his disposal, would give himself not the dose prescribed by medical rule for his malady but swallow all the medicine he could lay his hands on!

So much for traditional training and sophistic practice. Let us now glance at Plato's alternative. Plato in his search for human virtue turns from technical rules and other externalities, such as economic contracts and political compacts, to the inner nature of the human soul. Gradually he has come to construe education as the awakening of the inherent capacities of man.

Throughout the *Meno*, Socrates suggests, time after time, that virtue is not many but one. But he cannot make the Thessalian quite understand what he intends. Meno will divide virtue into parts, one befitting a man, another a woman, a master, a slave. In the *Republic*, Socrates states explicitly that virtue, as a unity, is the functioning of the human soul.

The virtuous soul is one which is active, healthy, normal. Things have functions, for example, an ear, a pruning-hook, a soul! The ear is virtuous when it hears, the pruning-hook when it cuts, the soul when it acts according to its complex nature. To inquire, then, whether virtue can be taught is to ask whether the capacities of human nature can be brought into actuality.

For Plato the soul of man is a living thing, and immortal. It acts in desire and in knowledge. By desire all men seek what is good. No one wishes evil for himself. When he does badly he has made a mistake; he has not known what to seek. The soul's faculties are three: appetite, passion or temper, and reason. To the first of these may be specifically assigned, by way of analysis, the virtue temperance; to the second, courage; to the third, wisdom. Justice or righteousness is the functioning of the whole soul with its parts in proper balance and proportion under the direction of reason. Without the control of this highest faculty incontinence and discontinuity will ensue, to the confusion and destruction in varying degrees of the life of the whole person. The doctrine of proportion is taken by way of analogy from medicine. There health is understood as the proper balance among the constituent elements of the organism, and the upsetting of apt proportion as the cause of abnormality.

Man through his endeavors may come to possess goods. He may, for instance, have fine appearance, wealth, temperance, courage. Theoretically the unlimited possession of very many types of good is possible, yet actually only one virtuous life is compossible. Good looks or wealth may destroy a man. The practice of temperance as a supreme virtue may impose narrowness, coldness, and self-righteousness of a negative sort. Courage, too, without the enlightenment and refinement of reason can issue in arrogance or brutality. The moral life is an organization in which many goods are put in their respective places in such a manner that the manifold capacities of the human organism are brought into a balanced activity, with all its faculties so disposed that none is destructive of the others.

This, then, is human virtue: how, now, is it to be "taught"? Plato's answer is to the effect that education has two parts and acts on two levels. At the lower level the pupil does not understand why he is being trained by the discipline he undertakes. Yet if this early training is sound, he will find on his attainment of adult discernment that what he has learned has already made him familiar with reason, which he will now recognize as a friend. The second and higher stage of education is the cultivation of intellectual activity. Here along with the content of training goes a comprehension of its means and ends.

The young, according to Plato, are like delicate green shoots which spring from nature. Their shapes may be set and their natures "hardened" into distorted and twisted trunks or into finely upright and well proportioned trees. To change the figure, children are volatile creatures without rhyme or reason. The latter metaphor is the more immediately apposite to Plato's description of early education. He would provide two means for their elementary training, namely, gymnastic and music. These the Greeks have long employed. Plato would modify traditional practice, by way of deletion and selection of texts, modes, and rhythms. Music includes literature. Its source is the early choral dance, in which text, gesture, and accompanying instrumentation are conjoined in a common representation of and commentary upon manners and morals. The more immediate purpose of gymnastic is the shaping of the body; that of music, discipline and dogma for the soul. Either, however, supplements the other, both producing order and co-ordination within the whole organism. The object of this double early training is habituated conduct. Habit, for Plato, is the basis of morality. Human beings become what they are by the repeated doing of what they do. The human organism is so constituted that through the repetition of any sort of act it assumes a corresponding mode of conduct.

Because this is the case, those who prescribe the details of elementary education should know what the natures of temperance, courage, justice, and other specific virtues are. This reflection by Plato introduces his scheme of higher education. In setting forth the latter he confronts his reader with the grave assertion that the educator can put nothing whatever into the soul of him who is to be taught. All he can do is elicit, through the presentation of appropriate objects, those inherent capacities which the soul contains. If training has already been bad, reform can be undertaken by turning the soul concerned to objects different from those previously entertained, so that the percipient may come to cognize these, if it be in his nature so to do. Every man's knowledge is his own. What he knows is that which in cognition proves appropriate to his nature.

To expose these conclusions Plato makes use of doctrines entertained by certain priests and priestesses, "wise" persons they who discern in their way the meaning of "possession." These people say that the soul of man, immortal as it is, inhabits many bodies in successive incarnations. Originally the soul has dwelt in a noetic world where it has beheld directly intelligible realities, *forms*. Because of its wrong-doing it has been consigned to the occupancy of bodies, and when enclosed in these it can perceive only dimly through the agency of sense and in remembrance those intelligible objects it has once clearly cognized.

The problem of knowledge on which the "wise" devotees of the "mysteries" throw light is brought into sharp focus by two statements within the *Meno*. The latter of these is seized upon by Socrates as the appropriate occasion for introducing an exhibition of intellectual cognition in the progress of learning by the Slave. The first is Meno's description of sense-experience as the commensurate functioning of a sense-organ and a sense-object. Plato is to extend this explanation in terms of perceptive commensurability to each stage of knowing, from sensation to cognition. Perception, he is to affirm, is the adjustment of an appropriate subject to an appropriate object. Opinion is a case in point. Here the object is a shadowy thing, somewhere between non-being and being, and the corresponding activity of the soul is neither ignorance nor knowledge. The percipient who relies upon opinions, however true they appear, will find that when put to the test, they have a way, like the famed statues of Daedalus, of deserting their bases. Only that knowledge is trustworthy which is secured by rational, logical consequences.

The second statement is a question of Meno's in the form of a popular "quibble": How can one inquire of anything? If he knows it, his inquiry is unnecessary; if he does not know it, how can he recognize it? Plato resolves the seeming paradox by having Socrates question the Slave. The latter has never studied mathematics; yet on the presentation before him by Socrates of diagrams drawn on the earth he is enabled to enunciate the proposition that the square on the square's diagonal is double the original figure. The Slave's procedure in learning this manifests three stages. It begins with a reliance on an "association" among numbers, passes through the error inherent in resultant opinion, and then arrives at necessary truth. His performance illustrates, according to Plato, the doctrine that knowledge is reminiscence, or, leaving aside the "mythology" of the "mysteries," that cognition is recognition. The Slave's sense-experience is not the cause of knowledge, but rather its occasion. Through the particular, which is in contact with sense, he discerns the underlying universal. Actually the squares drawn on the earth by Socrates are not squares at all. Their lines are not straight; their angles are distorted. Yet by means of these the Slave has been able to cognize the real, the universal square and to arrive at certain geometrical principles. In this case geometry is exemplary. The objects of all true knowledge, including those of moral wisdom, lie beyond the realm of sensible particulars. And even as the squares which are set before the Slave may be erased and yet squareness will remain, so no matter whether examples of temperance, courage, justice, and the like, are observed among men, these objects of cognition, the archetypes of virtuous conduct, exist and abide in a real world beyond the changing vicissitudes which belong to particulars in time and of place.

FULTON H. ANDERSON

SELECTED BIBLIOGRAPHY

Anderson, F. H., *The Argument of Plato*. London, 1934, pp. 6–56, 95–137.

Apelt, O., *Die mathematische Stelle im Menon*, Festschrift f. Th. Gomperz. Wien, 1902, pp. 290–97.

Burnet, J., *Greek Philosophy, Part I, Thales to Plato*. London, 1924, pp. 170–91.

Frazer, J. G., *The Growth of Plato's Ideal Theory*. London, 1930, pp. 41–80.

Gomperz, Th., *Greek Thinkers*. New York, 1905, II, pp. 367–78.

Grote, G., *Plato and Other Companions of Socrates*. London, 1867, II, pp. 1–28.

Robinson, R., *Plato's Earlier Dialectic*. Ithaca, 1941, pp. 7–20.

Shorey, P., *What Plato Said*. Chicago, 1933, pp. 155–59, 511–17.

Taylor, A. E., *Plato the Man and His Work*. New York, 1936, pp. 129–45.

Thompson, E. S., *The Meno of Plato*. London, 1901, pp. ix–lxvi.

MENO

MENO

CHARACTERS OF THE DIALOGUE

| MENO | A SLAVE OF MENO |
| SOCRATES | ANYTUS |

Meno. CAN you tell me, Socrates, whether virtue is acquired by teaching or by practice; or if neither by teaching nor practice, then whether it comes to man by nature, or in what other way?

Socrates. O Meno, there was a time when the Thessalians were famous among the other Hellenes only for their riches and their riding; but now, if I am not mistaken, they are equally famous for their wisdom, especially at Larissa, which is the native city of your friend Aristippus. And this is Gorgias' doing; for when he came there, the flower of the Aleuadae, among them your admirer Aristippus, and the other chiefs of the Thessalians, fell in love with his wisdom. And he has taught you the habit of answering questions in a grand and bold style, which becomes those who know, and is the style in which he himself answers all comers; and any Hellene who likes may ask him anything. How different is our lot! my dear Meno. Here at Athens, there is a dearth of the commodity, and all wisdom seems to have emigrated from us to you. I am certain that if you were to ask any Athenian whether virtue was natural or acquired, he would laugh in your face and say: "Stranger, you have far too good an opinion of me if you think that I can answer your question. For I literally do not know what virtue is, and much less whether it is acquired by teaching or not." And I myself, Meno, living as I do in this region of poverty, am as poor as the rest of the world, and I confess with shame that I know literally nothing about virtue;

and when I do not know the *"quid"* of anything, how can I know the *"quale"*? How, if I knew nothing at all of Meno, could I tell if he was fair or the opposite of fair; rich and noble, or the reverse of rich and noble? Do you think that I could?

Men. No, indeed. But are you in earnest, Socrates, in saying that you do not know what virtue is? And am I to carry back this report of you to Thessaly?

Soc. Not only that, my dear boy, but you may say further that I have never known of any one else who did, in my judgment.

Men. Then you have never met Gorgias when he was at Athens?

Soc. Yes, I have.

Men. And did you not think that he knew?

Soc. I have not a good memory, Meno, and therefore I cannot now tell what I thought of him at the time. And I dare say that he did know, and that you know what he said: please, therefore, do remind me of what he said; or, if you would rather, tell me your own view; for I suspect that you and he think much alike.

Men. Very true.

Soc. Then as he is not here, never mind him, and do you tell me: By the gods, Meno, be generous and tell me what you say that virtue is; for I shall be truly delighted to find that I have been mistaken, and that you and Gorgias do really have this knowledge, although I have been just saying that I have never found anybody who had.

Men. There will be no difficulty, Socrates, in answering your question. Let us take first the virtue of a man—he should know how to administer the state, and in the administration of it to benefit his friends and harm his enemies; and he must also be careful not to suffer harm himself. A woman's virtue, if you wish to know about that, may also be easily described: her duty is to order her house and keep what is indoors, and obey her husband. Every age, every condition of life, young or old, male or female, bond or free, has a different virtue: there are virtues numberless, and no lack of definitions of them; for

virtue is relative to the actions and ages of each of us in all
that we do. And the same may be said of vice, Socrates[1].

Soc. How fortunate I am, Meno! When I ask you for one
virtue, you present me with a swarm of them,[2] which are in
your keeping. Suppose that I carry on the figure of the swarm,
and ask of you, What is the nature of the bee? and you answer
that there are many kinds of bees, and I reply: But do bees
differ as bees because there are many and different kinds of
them; or are they not rather to be distinguished by some other
quality, as, for example, beauty, size, or shape? How would
you answer me?

Men. I should answer that bees do not differ from one another, as bees.

Soc. And if I went on to say: That is what I desire to know,
Meno; tell me what is the quality in which they do not differ,
but are all alike—would you be able to answer?

Men. I should.

Soc. And so of the virtues, however many and different they
may be, they have all a common nature which makes them
virtues; and on this he who would answer the question, "What
is virtue?" would do well to have his eye fixed; do you understand?

Men. I am beginning to understand; but I do not as yet
take hold of the question as I could wish.

Soc. When you say, Meno, that there is one virtue of a man,
another of a woman, another of a child, and so on, does this
apply only to virtue, or would you say the same of health, and
size, and strength? Or is the nature of health always the same,
whether in man or woman?

Men. I should say that health is the same, both in man and
woman.

Soc. And is not this true of size and strength? If a woman is
strong, she will be strong by reason of the same form and of
the same strength subsisting in her which there is in the man—

1 Cf. Arist. *Pol.* i. 13, § 10.
2 Cf. *Theaetetus* 146 D.

I mean to say that strength, as strength, whether of man or woman, is the same. Is there any difference?

Men. I think not.

Soc. And will not virtue, as virtue, be the same, whether in a child or in a grown-up person, in a woman or in a man?

Men. I cannot help feeling, Socrates, that this case is different from the others.

Soc. But why? Were you not saying that the virtue of a man was to order a state, and the virtue of a woman was to order a house?

Men. I did say so.

Soc. And can either house or state or anything be well ordered without temperance and without justice?

Men. Certainly not.

Soc. Then they who order a state or a house temperately or justly order them with temperance and justice?

Men. Certainly.

Soc. Then both men and women, if they are to be good men and women, must have the same virtues of temperance and justice?

Men. True.

Soc. And can either a young man or an elder one be good if they are intemperate and unjust?

Men. They cannot.

Soc. They must be temperate and just?

Men. Yes.

Soc. Then all men are good in the same way, and by participation in the same virtues?

Men. Such is the inference.

Soc. And they surely would not have been good in the same way unless their virtue had been the same?

Men. They would not.

Soc. Then now that the sameness of all virtue has been proven, try and remember what you and Gorgias say that virtue is.

Men. Will you have one definition of them all?

Soc. That is what I am seeking.

Men. If you want to have one definition of them all, I know not what to say but that virtue is the power of governing mankind.

Soc. And does this definition of virtue include all virtue? Is virtue the same in a child and in a slave, Meno? Can the child govern his father, or the slave his master; and would he who governed be any longer a slave?

Men. I think not, Socrates.

Soc. No, indeed; there would be small reason in that. Yet once more, fair friend; according to you, virtue is "the power of governing"; but do you not add "justly and not unjustly"?

Men. Yes, Socrates; I agree there; for justice is virtue.

Soc. Would you say "virtue," Meno, or "a virtue"?

Men. What do you mean?

Soc. I mean as I might say about anything; that a round, for example, is "a figure" and not simply "figure," and I should adopt this mode of speaking, because there are other figures.

Men. Quite right; and that is just what I am saying about virtue—that there are other virtues as well as justice.

Soc. What are they? Tell me the names of them, as I would tell you the names of the other figures if you asked me.

Men. Courage and temperance and wisdom and magnanimity are virtues; and there are many others.

Soc. Yes, Meno; and again we are in the same case: in searching after one virtue we have found many, though not in the same way as before; but we have been unable to find the common virtue which runs through them all.

Men. Why, Socrates, even now I am not able to follow you in the attempt to get at one common notion of virtue as of other things.

Soc. No wonder; but I will try to get nearer if I can, for you know that all things have a common notion. Suppose now that someone asked you the question which I asked before: Meno, he would say, what is figure? And if you answered "roundness," he would reply to you, in my way of speaking, by asking whether you would say that roundness is "figure" or "a figure"; and you would answer "a figure."

Men. Certainly.

Soc. And for this reason—that there are other figures?

Men. Yes.

Soc. And if he proceeded to ask, What other figures are there? you would have told him.

Men. I should.

Soc. And if he similarly asked what color is, and you answered whiteness, and the questioner rejoined, Would you say that whiteness is color or a color? you would reply, A color, because there are other colors as well.

Men. I should.

Soc. And if he had said, Tell me what they are?—you would have told him of other colors which are colors just as much as whiteness.

Men. Yes.

Soc. And suppose that he were to pursue the matter in my way, he would say: Ever and anon we are landed in particulars, but this is not what I want; tell me then, since you call them by a common name and say that they are all figures, even when opposed to one another, what is that common nature which you designate as figure—which contains straight as well as round, and is no more one than the other—that would be your mode of speaking?

Men. Yes.

Soc. And in speaking thus, you do not mean to say that the round is round any more than straight, or the straight any more straight than round?

Men. Certainly not.

Soc. You only assert that the round figure is not more a figure than the straight, or the straight than the round?

Men. Very true.

Soc. To what then do we give the name of figure? Try and answer. Suppose that when a person asked you this question either about figure or color, you were to reply, Man, I do not understand what you want, or know what you are saying; he would look rather astonished and say: Do you not understand that I am looking for the *"simile in multis"*? And then he might put the question in another form: Meno, he might say, what is that *"simile in multis"* which you call "figure," and which includes not only round and straight figures, but all? Could you not answer that question, Meno? I wish that you would try; the attempt will be good practice with a view to the answer about virtue.

Men. I would rather that you answer, Socrates.

Soc. Shall I indulge you?

Men. By all means.

Soc. And then you will tell me about virtue?

Men. I will.

Soc. Then I must do my best, for there is a prize to be won.

Men. Certainly.

Soc. Well, I will try and explain to you what figure is. What do you say to this answer?—Figure is the only thing which always follows color. Will you be satisfied with it, as I am sure that I should be if you would let me have a similar definition of virtue?

Men. But, Socrates, it is such a simple answer.

Soc. Why simple?

Men. Because, according to you, figure is that which always follows color.

(*Soc.* Granted.)

Men. But if a person were to say that he does not know what color is, any more than what figure is—what sort of answer would you have given him?

Soc. I should have told him the truth. And if he were a philosopher of the eristic and antagonistic sort, I should say to him: You have my answer, and if I am wrong, your business is to take up the argument and refute me. But if we were friends, and were talking as you and I are now, I should reply in a milder strain and more in the dialectician's vein; that is to say, I should not only speak the truth, but I should make use of premises which the person interrogated would be willing to admit. And this is the way in which I shall endeavor to approach you. You will acknowledge, will you not, that there is such a thing as an end, or termination, or extremity?—all which words I use in the same sense, although I am aware that Prodicus might draw distinctions about them; but still you, I am sure, would speak of a thing as ended or terminated—that is all which I am saying—not anything very difficult.

Men. Yes, I should; and I believe that I understand your meaning.

Soc. And you would speak of a surface and also of a solid, as for example in geometry.

Men. Yes.

Soc. Well then, you are now in a condition to understand my definition of figure. I define figure to be that in which the solid ends; or, more concisely, the limit of solid.

Men. And now, Socrates, what is color?

Soc. You are outrageous, Meno, in thus plaguing a poor old man to give you an answer, when you will not take the trouble of remembering what is Gorgias' definition of virtue.

Men. When you have told me what I ask, I will tell you, Socrates.

Soc. A man who was blindfolded has only to hear you talking, and he would know that you are a fair creature and have still many lovers.

Men. Why do you think so?

Soc. Why, because you always speak in imperatives; like all beauties when they are in their prime, you are tyrannical; and also, as I suspect, you have found out that I have a weakness for the fair, and therefore to humor you I must answer.

Men. Please do.

Soc. Would you like me to answer you after the manner of Gorgias, which is familiar to you?

Men. I should like nothing better.

Soc. Do not he and you and Empedocles say that there are certain effluences of existence?

Men. Certainly.

Soc. And passages into which and through which the effluences pass?

Men. Exactly.

Soc. And some of the effluences fit into the passages, and some of them are too small or too large?

Men. True.

Soc. And there is such a thing as sight?

Men. Yes.

Soc. And now, as Pindar says, "read my meaning": color is an effluence of form, commensurate with sight, and palpable to sense.

Men. That, Socrates, appears to me to be an admirable answer.

Soc. Why, yes, because it happens to be one which you have been in the habit of hearing: and your wit will have discovered, I suspect, that you may explain in the same way the nature of sound and smell, and of many other similar phenomena.

Men. Quite true.

Soc. The answer, Meno, was in the orthodox solemn vein, and therefore was more acceptable to you than the other answer about figure.

Men. Yes.

Soc. And yet, O son of Alexidemus, I cannot help thinking that the other was the better; and I am sure that you would be of the same opinion if you would only stay and be initiated, and were not compelled, as you said yesterday, to go away before the mysteries.

Men. But I will stay, Socrates, if you will give me many such answers.

Soc. Well then, for my own sake as well as for yours, I will do my very best; but I am afraid that I shall not be able to give you very many as good; and now, in your turn, you are to fulfill your promise, and tell me what virtue is in the universal; and do not make a singular into a plural, as the facetious say of those who break a thing, but deliver virtue to me whole and sound, and not broken into a number of pieces; I have given you the pattern.

Men. Well then, Socrates, virtue, as I take it, is when he,

who desires the honorable, is able to provide it for himself;
so the poet says, and I say, too—

Virtue is the desire of things honorable and the power of attaining
them.

Soc. And does he who desires the honorable also desire the
good?

Men. Certainly.

Soc. Then are there some who desire the evil and others who
desire the good? Do not all men, my dear sir, desire good?

Men. I think not.

Soc. There are some who desire evil?

Men. Yes.

Soc. Do you mean that they think the evils which they desire to be good; or do they know that they are evil and yet
desire them?

Men. Both, I think.

Soc. And do you really imagine, Meno, that a man knows
evils to be evils and desires them notwithstanding?

Men. Certainly I do.

Soc. And desire is of possession?

Men. Yes, of possession.

Soc. And does he think that the evils will do good to him
who possesses them, or does he know that they will do him
harm?

Men. There are some who think that the evils will do them
good, and others who know that they will do them harm.

Soc. And, in your opinion, do those who think that they
will do them good know that they are evils?

Men. Certainly not.

Soc. Is it not obvious that those who are ignorant of their
nature do not desire them; but they desire what they suppose
to be goods although they are really evils; and if they are
mistaken and suppose the evils to be goods, they really desire
goods?

Men. Yes, in that case.

Soc. Well, and do those who, as you say, desire evils, and think that evils are hurtful to the possessor of them, know that they will be hurt by them?

Men. They must know it.

Soc. And must they not suppose that those who are hurt are miserable in proportion to the hurt which is inflicted upon them?

Men. How can it be otherwise?

Soc. But are not the miserable ill fated?

Men. Yes, indeed.

Soc. And does anyone desire to be miserable and ill fated?

Men. I should say not, Socrates.

Soc. But if there is no one who desires to be miserable, there is no one, Meno, who desires evil; for what is misery but the desire and possession of evil?

Men. That appears to be the truth, Socrates, and I admit that nobody desires evil.

Soc. And yet, were you not saying just now that virtue is the desire and power of attaining good?

Men. Yes, I did say so.

Soc. But if this be affirmed, then the desire of good is common to all, and one man is no better than another in that respect?

Men. True.

Soc. And if one man is not better than another in desiring good, he must be better in the power of attaining it?

Men. Exactly.

Soc. Then, according to your definition, virtue would appear to be the power of attaining good?

Men. I entirely approve, Socrates, of the manner in which you now view this matter.

Soc. Then let us see whether what you say is true from another point of view; for very likely you may be right—you affirm virtue to be the power of attaining goods?

Men. Yes.

Soc. And the goods which you mean are such as health and

wealth and the possession of gold and silver, and having office and honor in the state—those are what you would call goods?

Men. Yes, I should include all those.

Soc. Then, according to Meno, who is the hereditary friend of the great king, virtue is the power of getting silver and gold; and would you add that they must be gained piously, justly, or do you deem this to be of no consequence? And is any mode of acquisition, even if unjust and dishonest, equally to be deemed virtue?

Men. Not virtue, Socrates, but vice.

Soc. Then justice or temperance or holiness, or some other part of virtue, as would appear, must accompany the acquisition, and without them the mere acquisition of good will not be virtue.

Men. Why, how can there be virtue without these?

Soc. And the non-acquisition of gold and silver in a dishonest manner for oneself or another; or, in other words, the want of them may be equally virtue?

Men. True.

Soc. Then the acquisition of such goods is no more virtue than the non-acquisition and want of them, but whatever is accompanied by justice or honesty is virtue, and whatever is devoid of justice is vice.

Men. It cannot be otherwise, in my judgment.

Soc. And were we not saying just now that justice, temperance, and the like, were each of them a part of virtue?

Men. Yes.

Soc. And so, Meno, this is the way in which you mock me.

Men. Why do you say that, Socrates?

Soc. Why, because I asked you to deliver virtue into my hands whole and unbroken, and I gave you a pattern according to which you were to frame your answer; and you have forgotten already and tell me that virtue is the power of attaining good justly, or with justice; and justice you acknowledge to be a part of virtue.

Men. Yes.

Soc. Then it follows from your own admissions that virtue

is doing what you do with a part of virtue; for justice and the like are said by you to be parts of virtue.

Men. What of that?

Soc. What of that! Why, did not I ask you to tell me the nature of virtue as a whole? And you are very far from telling me this, but declare every action to be virtue which is done with a part of virtue, as though you had told me and I must already know the whole of virtue, and this, too, when frittered away into little pieces. And, therefore, my dear Meno, I fear that I must begin again and repeat the same question: What is virtue? for otherwise I can only say that every action done with a part of virtue is virtue; what else is the meaning of saying that every action done with justice is virtue? Ought I not to ask the question over again; for can anyone who does not know virtue know a part of virtue?

Men. No; I do not say that he can.

Soc. Do you remember how, in the example of figure, we rejected any answer given in terms which were as yet unexplained or unadmitted?

Men. Yes, Socrates; and we were quite right in doing so.

Soc. But then, my friend, do not suppose that we can explain to anyone the nature of virtue as a whole through some unexplained portion of virtue, or anything at all in that fashion; we should only have to ask over again the old question, What is virtue? Am I not right?

Men. I believe that you are.

Soc. Then begin again, and answer me. What, according to you and your friend Gorgias, is the definition of virtue?

Men. O Socrates, I used to be told, before I knew you, that you were always doubting yourself and making others doubt; and now you are casting your spells over me, and I am simply getting bewitched and enchanted, and am at my wits' end. And if I may venture to make a jest upon you, you seem to me both in your appearance and in your power over others to be very like the flat torpedo fish, who torpifies those who come near him and touch him, as you have now torpified me, I think. For my soul and my tongue are really torpid, and I do not know how to answer you; and though I have been delivered of an infinite variety of speeches about virtue before now, and to many persons—and very good ones they were, as I thought—at this moment I cannot even say what virtue is. And I think that you are very wise in not voyaging and going away from home, for if you did in other places as you do in Athens, you would be cast into prison as a magician.

Soc. You are a rogue, Meno, and had all but caught me.

Men. What do you mean, Socrates?

Soc. I can tell why you made a simile about me.

Men. Why?

Soc. In order that I might make another simile about you. For I know that all pretty young gentlemen like to have pretty similes made about them—as well they may—but I shall not return the compliment. As to my being a torpedo, if the torpedo is torpid as well as the cause of torpidity in others, then indeed I am a torpedo, but not otherwise; for I perplex others, not because I am clear, but because I am utterly perplexed myself. And now I know not what virtue is, and you seem to be in the same case, although you did once perhaps know, before you touched me. However, I have no objection to join with you in the inquiry.

Men. And how will you inquire, Socrates, into that which you do not know? What will you put forth as the subject of inquiry? And if you find what you want, how will you ever know that this is the thing which you did not know?

Soc. I know, Meno, what you mean; but just see what a tiresome dispute you are introducing. You argue that a man cannot inquire either about that which he knows, or about that which he does not know; for if he knows, he has no need to inquire; and if not, he cannot; for he does not know the very subject about which he is to inquire.[3]

Men. Well, Socrates, and is not the argument sound?

Soc. I think not.

Men. Why not?

[3] Cf. Aristot. *Post. Anal.* I. i. 6.

Soc. I will tell you why: I have heard from certain wise men and women who spoke of things divine that—

Men. What did they say?

Soc. They spoke of a glorious truth, as I conceive.

Men. What was it and who were they?

Soc. Some of them were priests and priestesses who had studied how they might be able to give a reason of their profession; there have been poets also who spoke of these things by inspiration, like Pindar and many others who were inspired. And they say—mark now and see whether their words are true—they say that the soul of man is immortal, and at one time has an end, which is termed dying, and at another time is born again, but is never destroyed. And the moral is that a man ought to live always in perfect holiness. *"For in the ninth year Persephone sends the souls of those from whom she has received the penalty of ancient crime back again from beneath into the light of the sun above, and these are they who become noble kings and mighty men and great in wisdom and are called saintly heroes in after-ages."* The soul, then, as being immortal, and having been born again many times, and having seen all things that exist, whether in this world or in the world below, has knowledge of them all; and it is no wonder that she should be able to call to remembrance all that she ever knew about virtue and about everything; for as all nature is akin, and the soul has learned all things, there is no difficulty in her eliciting, or as men say "learning," out of a single recollection, all the rest, if a man is strenuous and does not faint; for all inquiry and all learning is but recollection. And therefore we ought not to listen to this sophistical argument about the impossibility of inquiry; for it will make us idle, and is sweet only to the sluggard; but the other saying will make us active and inquisitive. In that confiding, I will gladly inquire with you into the nature of virtue.

Men. Yes, Socrates; but what do you mean by saying that we do not learn, and that what we call learning is only a process of recollection? Can you teach me how this is?

Soc. I told you, Meno, just now that you were a rogue, and now you ask whether I can teach you, when I am saying that there is no teaching, but only recollection; and thus you imagine that you will involve me in a contradiction.

Men. Indeed, Socrates, I protest that I had no such intention. I only asked the question from habit; but if you can prove to me that what you say is true, I wish that you would.

Soc. It will be no easy matter, but I will try to please you to the utmost of my power. Suppose that you call one of your numerous attendants, that I may demonstrate on him.

Men. Certainly. Come hither, boy.

Soc. He is Greek, and speaks Greek, does he not?

Men. Yes, indeed; he was born in the house.

Soc. Attend now to the questions which I ask him, and observe whether he learns of me or only remembers.

Men. I will.

Soc. Tell me, boy, do you know that a figure like this is a square?

Boy. I do.

Soc. And you know that a square figure has these four lines equal?

Boy. Certainly.

Soc. And these lines which I have drawn through the middle of the square are also equal?

Boy. Yes.

Soc. A square may be of any size?

Boy. Certainly.

Soc. And if one side of the figure be of two feet, and the other side be of two feet, how much will the whole be? Let me explain: if in one direction the space was of two feet, and in the other direction of one foot, the whole would be of two feet taken once?

Boy. Yes.

Soc. But since this side is also of two feet, there are twice two feet?

Boy. There are.

Soc. Then the square is of twice two feet?

Boy. Yes.

Soc. And how many are twice two feet? Count and tell me.

Boy. Four, Socrates.

Soc. And might there not be another square twice as large as this, and having like this the lines equal?

Boy. Yes.

Soc. And of how many feet will that be?

Boy. Of eight feet.

Soc. And now try and tell the length of the line which forms the side of that double square: this is two feet—what will that be?

Boy. Clearly, Socrates, it will be double.

Soc. Do you observe, Meno, that I am not teaching the boy anything, but only asking him questions; and now he fancies that he knows how long a line is necessary in order to produce a figure of eight square feet; does he not?

Men. Yes.

Soc. And does he really know?

Men. Certainly not.

Soc. He only guesses that because the square is double, the line is double.

Men. True.

Soc. Observe him while he recalls the steps in regular order. (*To the Boy.*) Tell me, boy, do you assert that a double space comes from a double line? Remember that I am not speaking of an oblong, but of a figure equal every way, and twice the size of this—that is to say of eight feet; and I want to know whether you still say that a double square comes from a double line?

Boy. Yes.

Soc. But does not this line become doubled if we add another such line here?

Boy. Certainly.

Soc. And four such lines will make a space containing eight feet?

Boy. Yes.

Soc. Let us describe such a figure: Would you not say that this is the figure of eight feet?

Boy. Yes.

Soc. And are there not these four divisions in the figure, each of which is equal to the figure of four feet?

Boy. True.

Soc. And is not that four times four?

Boy. Certainly.

Soc. And four times is not double?

Boy. No, indeed.

Soc. But how much?

Boy. Four times as much.

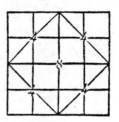

Soc. Therefore the double line, boy, has given a space, not twice, but four times as much.

Boy. True.

Soc. Four times four are sixteen—are they not?

Boy. Yes.

Soc. What line would give you a space of eight feet, as this gives one of sixteen feet—do you see?

Boy. Yes.

Soc. And the space of four feet is made from this half line?

Boy. Yes.

Soc. Good; and is not a space of eight feet twice the size of this, and half the size of the other?

Boy. Certainly.

Soc. Such a space, then, will be made out of a line greater than this one, and less than that one?

Boy. Yes, I think so.

Soc. Very good; I like to hear you say what you think. And now tell me, is not this a line of two feet and that of four?

Boy. Yes.

Soc. Then the line which forms the side of eight feet ought to be more than this line of two feet, and less than the other of four feet?

Boy. It ought.

Soc. Try and see if you can tell me how much it will be.

Boy. Three feet.

Soc. Then if we add a half to this line of two, that will be the line of three. Here are two and there is one; and on the other side, here are two also and there is one: and that makes the figure of which you speak?

Boy. Yes.

Soc. But if there are three feet this way and three feet that way, the whole space will be three times three feet?

Boy. That is evident.

Soc. And how much are three times three feet?

Boy. Nine.

Soc. And how much is the double of four?

Boy. Eight.

Soc. Then the figure of eight is not made out of a line of three?

Boy. No.

Soc. But from what line?—tell me exactly; and if you would rather not reckon, try and show me the line.

Boy. Indeed, Socrates, I do not know.

Soc. Do you see, Meno, what advances he has made in his power of recollection? He did not know at first, and he does not know now, what is the side of a figure of eight feet; but then he thought that he knew, and answered confidently as if he knew, and had no difficulty; now he has a difficulty, and neither knows nor fancies that he knows.

Men. True.

Soc. Is he not better off in knowing his ignorance?

Men. I think that he is.

Soc. If we have made him doubt, and given him the "torpedo's shock," have we done him any harm?

Men. I think not.

Soc. We have certainly, as would seem, assisted him in some degree to the discovery of the truth; and now he will wish to remedy his ignorance, but then he would have been ready to tell all the world again and again that the double space should have a double side.

Men. True.

Soc. But do you suppose that he would ever have inquired into or learned what he fancied that he knew, though he was really ignorant of it, until he had fallen into perplexity under the idea that he did not know, and had desired to know?

Men. I think not, Socrates.

Soc. Then he was the better for the torpedo's touch?

Men. I think so.

Soc. Mark now the further development. I shall only ask him, and not teach him, and he shall share the inquiry with me; and do you watch and see if you find me telling or explaining anything to him, instead of eliciting his opinion. Tell me, boy, is not this a square of four feet which I have drawn?

Boy. Yes.

Soc. And now I add another square equal to the former one?

Boy. Yes.

Soc. And a third, which is equal to either of them?

Boy. Yes.

Soc. Suppose that we fill up the vacant corner?

Boy. Very good.

Soc. Here, then, there are four equal spaces?

Boy. Yes.

Soc. And how many times larger is this space than this other?

Boy. Four times.

Soc. But it ought to have been twice only, as you will remember.

Boy. True.

Soc. And does not this line, reaching from corner to corner, bisect each of these spaces?

Boy. Yes.

Soc. And are there not here four equal lines which contain this space?

Boy. There are.

Soc. Look and see how much this space is.

Boy. I do not understand.

Soc. Has not each interior line cut off half of the four spaces?

Boy. Yes.

Soc. And how many spaces are there in this section?

Boy. Four.

Soc. And how many in this?

Boy. Two.

Soc. And four is how many times two?

Boy. Twice.

Soc. And this space is of how many feet?

Boy. Of eight feet.

Soc. And from what line do you get this figure?

Boy. From this.

Soc. That is, from the line which extends from corner to corner of the figure of four feet?

Boy. Yes.

Soc. And this is the line which the learned call the diagonal. And if this is the proper name, then you, Meno's slave, are prepared to affirm that the double space is the square of the diagonal?

Boy. Certainly, Socrates.

Soc. What do you say of him, Meno? Were not all these answers given out of his own head?

Men. Yes, they were all his own.

Soc. And yet, as we were just now saying, he did not know?

Men. True.

Soc. But still he had in him those notions of his—had he not?

Men. Yes.

Soc. Then he who does not know may still have true notions of that which he does not know?

Men. He has.

Soc. And at present these notions have just been stirred up in him, as in a dream; but if he were frequently asked the same questions, in different forms, he would know as well as anyone at last?

Men. I dare say.

Soc. Without anyone teaching him he will recover his knowledge for himself, if he is only asked questions?

Men. Yes.

Soc. And this spontaneous recovery of knowledge in him is recollection?

Men. True.

Soc. And this knowledge which he now has must he not either have acquired or always possessed?

Men. Yes.

Soc. But if he always possessed this knowledge he would always have known; or if he has acquired the knowledge he could not have acquired it in this life unless he has been taught geometry; for he may be made to do the same with all geometry and every other branch of knowledge. Now, has any one ever taught him all this? You must know about him if, as you say, he was born and bred in your house.

Men. And I am certain that no one ever did teach him.

Soc. And yet he has the knowledge?

Men. The fact, Socrates, is undeniable.

Soc. But if he did not acquire the knowledge in this life, then he must have had and learned it at some other time?

Men. Clearly he must.

Soc. Which must have been the time when he was not a man?

Men. Yes.

Soc. And if there have been always true thoughts in him, both at the time when he was and was not a man, which only need to be awakened into knowledge by putting questions to him, his soul must have always possessed this knowledge, for he always either was or was not a man?

Men. Obviously.

Soc. And if the truth of all things always existed in the soul, then the soul is immortal. Wherefore be of good cheer and try to recollect what you do not know, or rather what you do not remember.

Men. I feel, somehow, that I like what you are saying.

Soc. And I, Meno, like what I am saying. Some things I have said of which I am not altogether confident. But that we shall be better and braver and less helpless if we think that we ought to inquire than we should have been if we indulged in the idle fancy that there was no knowing and no use in seeking to know what we do not know—that is a theme upon which I am ready to fight, in word and deed, to the utmost of my power.

Men. There again, Socrates, your words seem to me excellent.

Soc. Then, as we are agreed that a man should inquire about that which he does not know, shall you and I make an effort to inquire together into the nature of virtue?

Men. By all means, Socrates. And yet I would much rather return to my original question, Whether in seeking to acquire virtue we should regard it as a thing to be taught, or as a gift of nature, or as coming to men in some other way?

Soc. Had I the command of you as well as of myself, Meno, I would not have inquired whether virtue is given by instruction or not, until we had first ascertained "what it is." But as you think only of controlling me who am your slave, and never of controlling yourself—such being your notion of freedom—I must yield to you, for you are irresistible. And therefore I have now to inquire into the qualities of a thing of which I do not as yet know the nature. At any rate, will you condescend a little and allow the question "Whether virtue is given by instruction, or in any other way," to be argued upon hypothesis? As the geometrician, when he is asked whether a certain triangle is capable of being inscribed in a certain circle[4], will reply: "I cannot tell you as yet, but I will offer a hypothesis which may assist us in forming a conclusion. If the figure be such that when you have produced a given side of it[5], the given area of the triangle falls short by an area corresponding to the part produced[6], then one consequence follows, and if this is impossible, then some other; and therefore I wish to assume a hypothesis before I tell you whether this triangle is capable of being inscribed in the circle"—that is a geometrical hypothesis. And we too, as we know not the nature and qualities of virtue, must ask whether virtue is or

4 Or: whether a certain area is capable of being inscribed as a triangle in a certain circle.

5 Or: when you apply it to the given line, i.e., the diameter of the circle (αὐτοῦ).

6 Or: similar to the area so applied.

is not taught, under a hypothesis: as thus, if virtue is of such a class of mental goods, will it be taught or not? Let the first hypothesis be that virtue is or is not knowledge—in that case will it be taught or not, or, as we were just now saying, "remembered"? For there is no use in disputing about the name. But is virtue taught or not, or rather, does not everyone see that knowledge alone is taught?

Men. I agree.

Soc. Then if virtue is knowledge, virtue will be taught?

Men. Certainly.

Soc. Then now we have made a quick end of this question: if virtue is of such a nature, it will be taught; and if not, not?

Men. Certainly.

Soc. The next question is whether virtue is knowledge or of another species?

Men. Yes, that appears to be the question which comes next in order.

Soc. Do we not say that virtue is a good?—This is a hypothesis which is not set aside.

Men. Certainly.

Soc. Now, if there be any sort of good which is distinct from knowledge, virtue may be that good; but if knowledge embraces all good, then we shall be right in thinking that virtue is knowledge?

Men. True.

Soc. And virtue makes us good?

Men. Yes.

Soc. And if we are good, then we are profitable; for all good things are profitable?

Men. Yes.

Soc. Then virtue is profitable?

Men. That is the only inference.

Soc. Then now let us see what are the things which severally profit us. Health and strength, and beauty and wealth—these, and the like of these, we call profitable?

Men. True.

Soc. And yet these things may also sometimes do us harm, would you not think so?

Men. Yes.

Soc. And what is the guiding principle which makes them profitable or the reverse? Are they not profitable when they are rightly used, and harmful when they are not rightly used?

Men. Certainly.

Soc. Next, let us consider the goods of the soul: they are temperance, justice, courage, quickness of apprehension, memory, magnanimity, and the like?

Men. Surely.

Soc. And such of these as are not knowledge, but of another sort, are sometimes profitable and sometimes hurtful; as, for example, courage wanting prudence, which is only a sort of confidence? When a man has no sense he is harmed by courage, but when he has sense he is profited?

Men. True.

Soc. And the same may be said of temperance and quickness of apprehension; whatever things are learned or done with sense are profitable, but when done without sense they are hurtful?

Men. Very true.

Soc. And in general, all that the soul attempts or endures, when under the guidance of wisdom, ends in happiness; but when she is under the guidance of folly, in the opposite?

Men. That appears to be true.

Soc. If then virtue is a quality of the soul, and is admitted to be profitable, it must be wisdom or prudence, since none of the things of the soul are either profitable or hurtful in themselves, but they are all made profitable or hurtful by the addition of wisdom or of folly; and therefore, if virtue is profitable, virtue must be a sort of wisdom or prudence?

Men. I quite agree.

Soc. And the other goods, such as wealth and the like, of which we were just now saying that they are sometimes good and sometimes evil, do not they also become profitable or hurtful, accordingly as the soul guides and uses them rightly or wrongly; just as the things of the soul herself are benefited when under the guidance of wisdom, and harmed by folly?

Men. True.

Soc. And the wise soul guides them rightly, and the foolish soul wrongly?

Men. Yes.

Soc. And is not this universally true of human nature? All other things hang upon the soul, and the things of the soul herself hang upon wisdom, if they are to be good; and so wisdom is inferred to be that which profits—and virtue, as we say, is profitable?

Men. Certainly.

Soc. And thus we arrive at the conclusion that virtue is either wholly or partly wisdom?

Men. I think that what you are saying, Socrates, is very true.

Soc. But if this is true, then the good are not by nature good?

Men. I think not.

Soc. If they had been, there would assuredly have been discerners of characters among us who would have known our future great men; and on their showing we should have adopted them, and when we had got them, we should have kept them in the citadel out of the way of harm, and set a stamp upon them far rather than upon a piece of gold, in order that no one might tamper with them; and when they grew up they would have been useful to the state?

Men. Yes, Socrates, that would have been the right way.

Soc. But if the good are not by nature good, are they made good by instruction?

Men. There appears to be no other alternative, Socrates. On the supposition that virtue is knowledge, there can be no doubt that virtue is taught.

Soc. Yes, indeed; but what if the supposition is erroneous?

Men. I certainly thought just now that we were right.

Soc. Yes, Meno; but a principle which has any soundness should stand firm not only just now, but always.

Men. Well; and why are you so slow of heart to believe that knowledge is virtue?

Soc. I will try and tell you why, Meno. I do not retract the assertion that if virtue is knowledge it may be taught; but I fear that I have some reason in doubting whether virtue is knowledge; for consider now and say whether virtue, and not only virtue but anything that is taught, must not have teachers and disciples?

Men. Surely.

Soc. And conversely, may not the art of which neither teachers nor disciples exist be assumed to be incapable of being taught?

Men. True; but do you think that there are no teachers of virtue?

Soc. I have certainly often inquired whether there were any, and taken great pains to find them, and have never succeeded; and many have assisted me in the search, and they were the persons whom I thought the most likely to know. Here at the moment when he is wanted we fortunately have sitting by us Anytus, the very person of whom we should make inquiry; to him then let us repair. In the first place, he is the son of a wealthy and wise father, Anthemion, who acquired his wealth, not by accident or gift, like Ismenias the Theban (who has recently made himself as rich as Polycrates), but by his own skill and industry, and who is a well-conditioned, modest man, not insolent, or overbearing, or annoying; moreover, this son of his has received a good education, as the Athenian people certainly appear to think, for they choose him to fill the highest offices. And these are the sort of men from whom you are likely to learn whether there are any teachers of virtue, and who they are. Please, Anytus, to help me and your friend Meno in answering our question, Who are the teachers? Consider the matter thus: If we wanted Meno to be a good physician, to whom should we send him? Should we not send him to the physicians?

Anytus. Certainly.

Soc. Or if we wanted him to be a good cobbler, should we not send him to the cobblers?

Any. Yes.

Soc. And so forth?

Any. Yes.

Soc. Let me trouble you with one more question. When we say that we should be right in sending him to the physicians if we wanted him to be a physician, do we mean that we should be right in sending him to those who profess the art rather than to those who do not, and to those who demand payment for teaching the art and profess to teach it to anyone who will come and learn? And if these were our reasons, should we not be right in sending him?

Any. Yes.

Soc. And might not the same be said of flute-playing and of the other arts? Would a man who wanted to make another a flute-player refuse to send him to those who profess to teach the art for money, and be plaguing other persons to give him instruction, who are not professed teachers and who never had a single disciple in that branch of knowledge which he wishes him to acquire—would not such conduct be the height of folly?

Any. Yes, by Zeus, and of ignorance, too.

Soc. Very good. And now you are in a position to advise with me about my friend Meno. He has been telling me, Anytus, that he desires to attain that kind of wisdom and virtue by which men order the state or the house, and honor their parents, and know when to receive and when to send away citizens and strangers, as a good man should. Now, to whom should he go in order that he may learn this virtue? Does not the previous argument imply clearly that we should send him to those who profess and avouch that they are the common teachers of all Hellas, and are ready to impart instruction to anyone who likes, at a fixed price?

Any. Whom do you mean, Socrates?

Soc. You surely know, do you not, Anytus, that these are the people whom mankind call Sophists?

Any. By Heracles, Socrates, forebear! I only hope that no friend or kinsman or acquaintance of mine, whether citizen or stranger, will ever be so mad as to allow himself to be corrupted by them; for they are a manifest pest and corrupting influence to those who have to do with them.

Soc. What, Anytus? Of all the people who profess that they know how to do men good, do you mean to say that these are the only ones who not only do them no good, but positively corrupt those who are entrusted to them, and in return for this disservice have the face to demand money? Indeed, I cannot believe you; for I know of a single man, Protagoras, who made more out of his craft than the illustrious Phidias, who created such noble works, or any ten other statuaries. How could that be? A mender of old shoes, or patcher-up of clothes, who made the shoes or clothes worse than he received them, could not have remained thirty days undetected, and would very soon have starved; whereas, during more than forty years, Protagoras was corrupting all Hellas and sending his disciples from him worse than he received them, and he was never found out. For, if I am not mistaken, he was about seventy years old at his death, forty of which were spent in the practice of his profession; and during all that time he had a good reputation, which to this day he retains: and not only Protagoras, but many others are well spoken of; some who lived before him, and others who are still living. Now, when you say that they deceived and corrupted the youth, are they to be supposed to have corrupted them consciously or unconsciously? Can those who were deemed by many to be the wisest men of Hellas have been out of their minds?

Any. Out of their minds! No, Socrates, the young men who gave their money to them were out of their minds; and their relations and guardians who entrusted their youth to the care of these men were still more out of their minds, and most of all, the cities who allowed them to come in, and did not drive them out, citizen and stranger alike.

Soc. Has any of the Sophists wronged you, Anytus? What makes you so angry with them?

Any. No, indeed, neither I nor any of my belongings has ever had, nor would I suffer them to have, anything to do with them.

Soc. Then you are entirely unacquainted with them?

Any. And I have no wish to be acquainted.

Soc. Then, my dear friend, how can you know whether a thing is good or bad of which you are wholly ignorant?

Any. Quite well; I am sure that I know what manner of men these are, whether I am acquainted with them or not.

Soc. You must be a diviner, Anytus, for I really cannot make out, judging from your own words, how, if you are not acquainted with them, you know about them. But I am not inquiring of you who are the teachers who will corrupt Meno (let them be, if you please, the Sophists); I only ask you to tell him who there is in this great city who will teach him how to become eminent in the virtues which I was just now describing. He is the friend of your family, and you will oblige him.

Any. Why do you not tell him yourself?

Soc. I have told him whom I supposed to be the teachers of these things; but I learn from you that I am utterly at fault, and I dare say that you are right. And now I wish that you, on your part, would tell me to whom among the Athenians he should go. Whom would you name?

Any. Why single out individuals? Any Athenian gentleman, taken at random, if he will mind him, will do far more good to him than the Sophists.

Soc. And did those gentlemen grow of themselves; and without having been taught by anyone, were they nevertheless able to teach others that which they had never learned themselves?

Any. I imagine that they learned of the previous generation of gentlemen. Have there not been many good men in this city?

Soc. Yes, certainly, Anytus; and many good statesmen also there always have been, and there are still, in the city of Athens. But the question is whether they were also good teachers of their own virtue—not whether there are, or have been, good men in this part of the world, but whether virtue can be taught, is the question which we have been discussing. Now, do we mean to say that the good men of our own and of other times knew how to impart to others that virtue which they had themselves; or is virtue a thing incapable of being communicated or imparted by one man to another? That is the question which I and Meno have been arguing. Look at the matter in your own way: Would you not admit that Themistocles was a good man?

Any. Certainly; no man better.

Soc. And must not he then have been a good teacher, if any man ever was a good teacher, of his own virtue?

Any. Yes, certainly—if he wanted to be so.

Soc. But would he not have wanted? He would, at any rate, have desired to make his own son a good man and a gentleman; he could not have been jealous of him, or have intentionally abstained from imparting to him his own virtue. Did you never hear that he made his son Cleophantus a famous horseman; and had him taught to stand upright on horseback and hurl a javelin, and to do many other marvelous things; and in anything which could be learned from a master he was well trained? Have you not heard from our elders of him?

Any. I have.

Soc. Then no one could say that his son showed any want of capacity?

Any. Very likely not.

Soc. But did anyone, old or young, ever say in your hearing that Cleophantus, son of Themistocles, was a wise or good man, as his father was?

Any. I have certainly never heard anyone say so.

Soc. And if virtue could have been taught, would his father Themistocles have sought to train him in these minor accomplishments, and allowed him who, as you must remember, was his own son, to be no better than his neighbors in those qualities in which he himself excelled?

Any. Indeed, indeed, I think not.

Soc. Here was a teacher of virtue whom you admit to be among the best men of the past. Let us take another—Aristides, the son of Lysimachus; would you not acknowledge that he was a good man?

Any. To be sure I should.

Soc. And did not he train his son Lysimachus better than any other Athenian in all that could be done for him by the help of masters? But what has been the result? Is he a bit better than any other mortal? He is an acquaintance of yours, and you see what he is like. There is Pericles, again, magnificent in his wisdom; and he, as you are aware, had two sons, Paralus and Xanthippus.

Any. I know.

Soc. And you know, also, that he taught them to be unrivaled horsemen, and had them trained in music and gymnastics and all sorts of arts—in these respects they were on a level with the best—and had he no wish to make good men of them? Nay, he must have wished it. But virtue, as I suspect, could not be taught. And that you may not suppose the incompetent teachers to be only the meaner sort of Athenians and few in number, remember again that Thucydides had two sons, Melesias and Stephanus, whom, besides giving them a good education in other things, he trained in wrestling, and they were the best wrestlers in Athens: one of them he committed to the care of Xanthias, and the other to Eudorus, who had the reputation of being the most celebrated wrestlers of that day. Do you remember them?

Any. I have heard of them.

Soc. Now, can there be a doubt that Thucydides, whose children were taught things for which he had to spend money, would have taught them to be good men, which would have cost him nothing, if virtue could have been taught? Will you reply that he was a mean man, and had not many friends among the Athenians and allies? Nay, but he was of a great family, and a man of influence at Athens and in all Hellas, and, if virtue could have been taught, he would have found out some Athenian or foreigner who would have made good men of his sons if he could not himself spare the time from cares of state. Once more, I suspect, friend Anytus, that virtue is not a thing which can be taught.

Any. Socrates, I think that you are too ready to speak evil of men: and, if you will take my advice, I would recommend you to be careful. Perhaps there is no city in which it is not easier to do men harm than to do them good, and this is certainly the case at Athens, as I believe that you know.

Soc. O Meno, I think that Anytus is in a rage. And he may well be in a rage, for he thinks, in the first place, that I am defaming these gentlemen; and in the second place, he is of opinion that he is one of them himself. But some day he will know what is the meaning of defamation, and if he ever does, he will forgive me. Meanwhile I will return to you, Meno; for I suppose that there are gentlemen in your region, too?

Men. Certainly there are.

Soc. And are they willing to teach the young, and do they profess to be teachers, and do they agree that virtue is taught?

Men. No, indeed, Socrates, they are anything but agreed; you may hear them saying at one time that virtue can be taught, and then again the reverse.

Soc. Can we call those "teachers" who do not acknowledge the possibility of their own vocation?

Men. I think not, Socrates.

Soc. And what do you think of these Sophists, who are the only professors? Do they seem to you to be teachers of virtue?

Men. I often wonder, Socrates, that Gorgias is never heard promising to teach virtue; and when he hears others promising he only laughs at them, but he thinks that men should be taught to speak.

Soc. Then do you not think that the Sophists are teachers?

Men. I cannot tell you, Socrates; like the rest of the world, I am in doubt, and sometimes I think that they are teachers, and sometimes not.

Soc. And are you aware that not you only and other politicians have doubts whether virtue can be taught or not, but that Theognis the poet says the very same thing?

Men. Where does he say so?

Soc. In these elegiac verses:

Eat and drink and sit with the mighty, and make yourself agreeable to them; for from the good you will learn what is good, but if you mix with the bad, you will lose the intelligence which you already have.[7]

---

[7] Theog. 33 ff.

Do you observe that here he seems to imply that virtue can be taught?

Men. Clearly.

Soc. But in some other verses he shifts about and says: [8]

If understanding could be created and put into a man, then they [who were able to perform this feat] would have obtained great rewards.

And again:

Never would a bad son have sprung from a good sire, for he would have heard the voice of instruction; but not by teaching will you ever make a bad man into a good one.

And this, as you may remark, is a contradiction of the other.

Men. Clearly.

Soc. And is there anything else of which the professors are affirmed not only not to be teachers of others, but to be ignorant themselves, and bad at the knowledge of that which they are professing to teach; or is there anything about which even the acknowledged "gentlemen" are sometimes saying that "this thing can be taught," and sometimes the opposite? Can you say that they are teachers in any true sense whose ideas are in such confusion?

Men. I should say, certainly not.

Soc. But if neither the Sophists nor the gentlemen are teachers, clearly there can be no other teachers?

Men. No.

Soc. And if there are no teachers, neither are there disciples?

Men. Agreed.

Soc. And we have admitted that a thing cannot be taught of which there are neither teachers nor disciples?

Men. We have.

Soc. And there are no teachers of virtue to be found anywhere?

Men. There are not.

8 *Ibid.* 435 ff.

Soc. And if there are no teachers, neither are there scholars?

Men. That, I think, is true.

Soc. Then virtue cannot be taught?

Men. Not if we are right in our view. But I cannot believe, Socrates, that there are no good men; and if there are, how did they come into existence?

Soc. I am afraid, Meno, that you and I are not good for much, and that Gorgias has been as poor an educator of you as Prodicus has been of me. Certainly we shall have to look to ourselves, and try to find someone who will help in some way or other to improve us. This I say, because I observe that in the previous discussion none of us remarked that right and good action is possible to man under other guidance than that of knowledge (ἐπιστήμη)—and indeed if this be denied, there is no seeing how there can be any good men at all.

Men. How do you mean, Socrates?

Soc. I mean that good men are necessarily useful or profitable. Were we not right in admitting this? It must be so.

Men. Yes.

Soc. And in supposing that they will be useful only if they are true guides to us of action—there we were also right?

Men. Yes.

Soc. But when we said that a man cannot be a good guide unless he has knowledge (φρόνησις), in this we were wrong.

Men. What do you mean by the word "right"?

Soc. I will explain. If a man knew the way to Larisa, or anywhere else, and went to the place and led others thither, would he not be a right and good guide?

Men. Certainly.

Soc. And a person who had a right opinion about the way, but had never been and did not know, might be a good guide also, might he not?

Men. Certainly.

Soc. And while he has true opinion about that which the other knows, he will be just as good a guide if he thinks the truth, as he who knows the truth?

Men. Exactly.

Soc. Then true opinion is as good a guide to correct action as knowledge; and that was the point which we omitted in our speculation about the nature of virtue, when we said that knowledge only is the guide of right action; whereas there is also right opinion.

Men. True.

Soc. Then right opinion is not less useful than knowledge?

Men. The difference, Socrates, is only that he who has knowledge will always be right; but he who has right opinion will sometimes be right, and sometimes not.

Soc. What do you mean? Can he be wrong who has right opinion, so long as he has right opinion?

Men. I admit the cogency of your argument, and therefore, Socrates, I wonder that knowledge should be preferred to right opinion—or why they should ever differ.

Soc. And shall I explain this wonder to you?

Men. Do tell me.

Soc. You would not wonder if you had ever observed the images of Daedalus [9]; but perhaps you have not got them in your country?

Men. What have they to do with the question?

Soc. Because they require to be fastened in order to keep them, and if they are not fastened, they will play truant and run away.

Men. Well, what of that?

Soc. I mean to say that they are not very valuable possessions if they are at liberty, for they will walk off like runaway slaves; but when fastened, they are of great value, for they are really beautiful works of art. Now this is an illustration of the nature of true opinions: while they abide with us they are beautiful and fruitful, but they run away out of the human soul, and do not remain long, and therefore they are not of much value until they are fastened by the tie of the cause; and this fastening of them, friend Meno, is recollection, as you and I have agreed to call it. But when they are bound, in

[9] Cf. *Euthyphro* 11b.

the first place, they have the nature of knowledge; and, in the second place, they are abiding. And this is why knowledge is more honorable and excellent than true opinion, because fastened by a chain.

Men. What you are saying, Socrates, seems to be very like the truth.

Soc. I, too, speak rather in ignorance; I only conjecture. And yet that knowledge differs from true opinion is no matter of conjecture with me. There are not many things which I profess to know, but this is most certainly one of them.

Men. Yes, Socrates; and you are quite right in saying so.

Soc. And am I not also right in saying that true opinion leading the way perfects action quite as well as knowledge?

Men. There again, Socrates, I think you are right.

Soc. Then right opinion is not a whit inferior to knowledge, or less useful in action; nor is the man who has right opinion inferior to him who has knowledge?

Men. True.

Soc. And surely the good man has been acknowledged by us to be useful?

Men. Yes.

Soc. Seeing then that men become good and useful to states, not only because they have knowledge, but because they have right opinion, and that neither knowledge nor right opinion is given to man by nature or acquired by him—(do you imagine either of them to be given by nature?

Men. Not I.)

Soc. Then if they are not given by nature, neither are the good by nature good?

Men. Certainly not.

Soc. And nature being excluded, then came the question whether virtue is acquired by teaching?

Men. Yes.

Soc. If virtue was widom [or knowledge], then, as we thought, it was taught?

Men. Yes.

Soc. And if it was taught, it was wisdom?

Men. Certainly.

Soc. And if there were teachers, it might be taught; and if there were no teachers, not?

Men. True.

Soc. But surely we acknowledged that there were no teachers of virtue?

Men. Yes.

Soc. Then we acknowledged that it was not taught, and was not wisdom.

Men. Certainly.

Soc. And yet we admitted that it was a good?

Men. Yes.

Soc. And the right guide is useful and good?

Men. Certainly.

Soc. And the only right guides are knowledge and true opinion—these are the guides of man; for things which happen by chance are not under the guidance of man; but the guides of man are true opinion and knowledge.

Men. I think so, too.

Soc. But if virtue is not taught, neither is virtue knowledge.

Men. Clearly not.

Soc. Then of two good and useful things, one, which is knowledge, has been set aside and cannot be supposed to be our guide in political life.

Men. I think not.

Soc. And therefore not by any wisdom, and not because they were wise, did Themistocles and those others of whom Anytus spoke govern states. This was the reason why they were unable to make others like themselves—because their virtue was not grounded on knowledge.

Men. That is probably true, Socrates.

Soc. But if not by knowledge, the only alternative which remains is that statesmen must have guided states by right opinion, which is in politics what divination is in religion; for diviners and also prophets say many things truly, but they know not what they say.

Men. So I believe.

Soc. And may we not, Meno, truly call those men "divine" who, having no understanding, yet succeed in many a grand deed and word?

Men. Certainly.

Soc. Then we shall also be right in calling divine those whom we were just now speaking of as diviners and prophets, including the whole tribe of poets. Yes, and statesmen above all may be said to be divine and illumined, being inspired and possessed of the god, in which condition they say many grand things, not knowing what they say.

Men. Yes.

Soc. And the women, too, Meno, call good men divine—do they not? And the Spartans, when they praise a good man, say "that he is a divine man."

Men. And I think, Socrates, that they are right, although very likely our friend Anytus may take offense at the word.

Soc. I do not care; as for Anytus, there will be another opportunity of talking with him. To sum up our inquiry—the result seems to be, if we are at all right in our view, that virtue is neither natural nor acquired, but an instinct given by God to the virtuous. Nor is the instinct accompanied by reason, unless there may be supposed to be among statesmen someone who is capable of educating statesmen. And if there be such a one, he may be said to be among the living what Homer says that Tiresias was among the dead, "he alone has understanding; but the rest are flitting shades"; and he and his virtue in like manner will be a reality among shadows.

Men. That is excellent, Socrates.

Soc. Then, Meno, the conclusion is that virtue comes to the virtuous by divine dispensation. But we shall never know the certain truth until, before asking how virtue is given, we inquire into the actual nature of virtue. I fear that I must go away, but do you, now that you are persuaded yourself, persuade our friend Anytus. And do not let him be so exasperated; if you can conciliate him, you will have done good service to the Athenian people.

The Library of Liberal Arts